EVERY D[...]

with Jes[...]

EXPLORING THE [...]

RUTH & ESTHER
When Sovereignty Surprises

BY SELWYN HUGHES

QUIET TIME

Almighty God,
great and
majestic,
I know that You encircle the
needs of your children
with the broad embrace of
eternal solution.
But Abba Father,
do not leave me
struggling and unstroked
upon this earth!
If grace has a lap,
find and hold me there till
all my cries and longings
snuggle at last into the
Arms of Peace.

I BELONG

For Reading and Meditation: Matthew 1:1–17

"Boaz the father of Obed, whose mother was Ruth ..." (v. 5)

Our theme for this edition centres on the only two books in the Bible which are named after women – Esther and Ruth. Although the two books are quite different in style and scope, there are several intriguing similarities. Consider, as we begin, some of the more obvious of these. First, both books depict a woman who was brought by God into an unusual marriage. Second, both books are set against a background of great national peril. Third, both books teach us valuable lessons about the providential dealings of a great and loving God.

We focus first on the story of Ruth, and then later we shall examine the life and times of the godly Queen Esther. The first thing we must notice about Ruth is that her name is included in Matthew's genealogy of our Lord Jesus Christ. It was the custom in Israel when writing out a genealogy to list only the names of men, but occasionally, if there was a special reason to do so, the names of women were included. Good and godly though Ruth was, however, the real reason why her name is mentioned here is because she was among those who were the direct antecedents of the Lord Jesus Christ. She, as well as the others, are given prominence not because of what they had achieved but because of who they were related to – Jesus.

You are who you are because He is who He is.

It is a parable. Our real greatness in this world arises not so much from what we do but from whether or not we are directly related to Christ. When we are linked by faith to Him we are given a status that lifts us above the greatest of earth's categories. This is where real significance lies – in being related to Him. Never forget – you are who you are because He is who He is.

O Father, how can I ever thank You enough for bringing me into a relationship with Yourself and with Your Son? I belong – belong to You and thus to everyone else who belongs to You. I am so deeply, deeply grateful. Amen.

THE DANGER OF EXPEDIENCY

For Reading and Meditation: Ruth 1:1–2

"A man ... together with his wife and two sons, went to live ... in the country of Moab." (v. 1)

Because of the famine which was ravaging Israel, Elimelech and his little family make the decision to emigrate to the land of Moab. Was this a right decision – or a wrong one? Bible students have debated this question for centuries. You must decide for yourself, but first consider the facts.

The Moabites were the result of the incestuous union between Lot and his daughters (Gen. 19:29–38). They appeared to be a bad bunch who always opposed Israel. On one occasion they refused the Israelites bread and water, and hired Balaam to curse them. Because of this, God forbade the Moabites to come into the presence of the Lord, and told the Israelites not to seek their peace or their prosperity (Deut. 23:3–7).

Elimelech's decision to move his family into Moab may have appeared to be a good choice economically, but I believe it was a bad choice spiritually. He went directly against God's commands. Of course, it can be argued that when one considers the positive things that came out of the move – the book of Ruth for example – then what they did was right. But when we see good coming out of something, we must never assume that God willed it that way; rather, He works through the bad to make all things contribute to His glory. Christians should never try to foresee the results of an action and thus justify going against God's commands. Instead, it should be the constant practice of every Christian to decide everything on the basis of God's will as displayed in His Word. We live dangerously when we allow expediency, and not the clear guidelines of Scripture, to determine our actions and our directions.

God works through the bad to make all things contribute to His glory.

O Father, burn into my consciousness the things I have read today so that I will never be directed by expediency but by the clear directions that come out of Your Word. In Jesus' Name I ask it. Amen.

PUTTING GOD FIRST

For Reading and Meditation: Ruth 1:3–5

"Now Elimelech, Naomi's husband, died, and she was left with her two sons." (v. 3)

Although Elimelech's decision to care and provide for his family must be applauded, there can be little doubt that in moving to the land of Moab he went against the will of God. Everything seemed to go well at first, and no doubt the improved economic conditions were to their liking. One day, however, tragedy strikes. Elimelech is taken ill and dies. Naomi, his wife, now faces the devastation of bereavement. Later, her two sons – both of whom had taken Moabite wives – also die, and she has to bear the pain of this further tragedy. These circumstances reinforce the point we made yesterday about the folly of making decisions based on expediency rather than on the will of God. How prone we are to allow materialistic or economic values to influence our judgement.

A letter in my mail tells of a man and his family who emigrated to another country, lured by the appeal of financial security. He wrote: "Would to God I had thought of the spiritual implications before I made the move. My life and family are in ruins." This is why it is always wise to pray over a move to another town, city or country, as there may be unseen dangers that are revealed only through prayer.

A change of circumstances will not necessarily solve our problems. We think if we had a new home, a new church, a new husband or wife, a new minister, or a new job, that all our difficulties would be over. As Christians, every major decision we make ought to be set against God's perfect will. We owe it to God to bring Him into our decision making. Otherwise we may find we have gained economically but lost out spiritually.

The folly of making decisions based on expediency rather than on the will of God.

My Father and my God, help me never to allow economic or personal considerations to influence my judgement when making life's major decisions. Grant that I might subject all my decisions and movements to Your perfect will. In Jesus' Name. Amen.

FORGIVE YOURSELF!
For Reading and Meditation: Ruth 1:6–13

*"Naomi and her daughters-in-law
prepared to return home." (v. 6)*

After Naomi has recovered from the shock of losing her husband and two sons in the land of Moab, she hears that Israel is once again a flourishing land and she makes up her mind to return to her people. When she announces her intentions to her daughters-in-law, Ruth and Orpah, they decide to accompany her on the journey home. As the three make their way out of Moab, Naomi feels it necessary to point out to the young women that their chances of finding someone to marry in Canaan would be very remote. What mother in Israel would allow her son to marry a woman from Moab? Naomi makes it clear that if she had other sons who were eligible for marriage, she would gladly give them to her two bereaved daughters-in-law, but as this is not so she encourages them to return to their own homes.

At this point Naomi seems saddened and overwhelmed by all that has happened and utters these solemn words: "It is more bitter for me than for you, because the Lord's hand has gone out against me" (v. 13). We must be careful not to read too much into this statement, but I cannot help but feel that there were some feelings of self-recrimination and self-contempt reverberating beneath that remark. Naomi, being an Israelite, would have known how to approach God for forgiveness. However, it would appear from the remark she makes that she has not yet forgiven herself.

Self-pity and self-contempt are always signals that say one has not really received the divine forgiveness. Whenever you are in need of forgiveness, open your soul to receive it, and then make sure you do not short-circuit the spiritual system by failing to forgive yourself.

Whenever you are in need of forgiveness, open your soul to receive it.

Heavenly Father, I see how easy it is to allow sorrow for my sin to become self-reproach or self-pity. Help me, whenever I am in need of forgiveness, to receive it from You, and then to forgive myself. In Jesus' Name I pray. Amen.

THE LEAP OF FAITH

For Reading and Meditation: Ruth 1:14–18

*"Where you go I will go,
and where you stay I will stay." (v. 16)*

Afterwards Naomi's advice to her daughters-in-law that they should stay in Moab, Orpah, albeit reluctantly prepares to return home. Ruth, however, has other ideas. So deep is her love for her mother-in-law that she begs to be allowed to accompany her to Israel. She pleads her case in what is without doubt one of the most moving passages in the Old Testament.

Ruth is well aware that great problems will face her when she arrives in Israel – national, cultural and religious. But her determination to remain at the side of her mother-in-law is so great that she pours out her feelings in these words: "Where you go I will go, and where you stay I will stay." Such is her love for Naomi that the possibility that they might have no permanent home makes no difference whatsoever. "Your people will be my people." Imagine giving up your friends and family to settle in a land where you know you could well be ostracized. "And your God my God." Ruth had evidently seen and heard enough from Naomi to realise that the God of the Israelites was Someone worth knowing. The true Deity was vastly superior to the non-existent "deities" of Moab.

What a magnificent picture this is of a true conversion. Ruth and Orpah stand at the crossroads. Orpah draws back to end her days in the darkness of heathen idolatry, while Ruth moves on to a new land and a new future, and to have her name inscribed for ever on the sacred record. How sad that so many can appear to be deeply religious, travel for a time with God's people, yet fail to make that "leap of faith" that entrust all one has and all one is to the Saviour. If you have not done so, make the leap of faith today.

If you have not done so, make the leap of faith today.

Gracious and loving Father, help me understand that keeping company with Your people is not enough for salvation. I must make that determined leap of faith. I do so now. Receive me and make me Yours. In Jesus' Name. Amen.

THE MARKS OF DISOBEDIENCE
For Reading and Meditation: Ruth 1:19–22

"The Lord has afflicted me; the Almighty has brought misfortune upon me." (v. 21)

After the long journey from Moab, Naomi, in company with her daughter-in-law, Ruth, finally reaches Bethlehem. There she is welcomed by the whole community, who seemingly turn out in force to greet her.

One can deduce from the question "Can this be Naomi?" (v. 19) something of the change that must have taken place in her appearance. Undoubtedly, the circumstances through which she had passed, and the sojourn in Moab, had left deep marks upon her. Naomi's response is swift, and still tinged with self-recrimination: "Don't call me Naomi [sweet or pleasant] ... Call me Mara, [unpleas-ant] because the Almighty has made my life very bitter." Although, as we said yesterday, there might have been some feelings of self-recrimination in Naomi's heart, the fact must not be overlooked that she was also a living testimony of what happens to those who choose some way other than God's way. "Those who take God's way," says Dr E. Stanley Jones, "get results. Those who don't get consequences."

I have met many in my time who stepped out of the will of God, and although they returned to Him and were forgiven, they still carry in their bodies and personalities the consequences of their actions. Just recently I heard of a Christian, who, finding he had homosexual tendencies, decided to engage in one homosexual encounter – just to see what it would be like. He contracted Aids, and unless the Lord heals him or a cure is found, he will probably die. We ought to remember that if we move away from the will of God, the sin in which we engage can be forgiven, but the marks of sin may remain in us and upon us for a lifetime.

"Those who take God's way get results. Those who don't get consequences."

Father, I see that in this world I can either get results – or consequences. Help me not to go against the grain of the universe, for life is designed to move in one way – Your way. Teach me to walk in Your statutes. Amen.

MAXIMISING TIME

For Reading and Meditation: Ruth 2:1–3

*"Naomi had a relative on her husband's side...
a man of standing, whose name was Boaz." (v. 1)*

Verse 1 tells us that Naomi's deceased husband, Elimelech, came from a wealthy family, and that now most of that wealth was in the hands of a young relative of Elimelech's – Boaz.

Naomi and Ruth have arrived in Bethlehem just as the harvest is about to begin and Ruth, being the kind of woman she is, sets about the task of finding something to do. People of character always have a mind to work. Continued laziness, unless physiologically based, is evidence that a person's character is flawed. He or she is non-contributive and thus will not discover that "It is more blessed to give than to receive."

At harvest time there was always work to be found in the fields, even if it was only gathering up after the reapers. When the workers went through the fields reaping the harvest, often, because of the speed at which they worked, they would leave behind small unreaped sections. These unreaped areas were then covered by "gleaners", who would walk behind and reap the grain that was still standing. Jewish law stated that the gleanings must be left for the poor and the grain collected by the gleaners became theirs (Lev. 19:9–10; Deut. 24:19). During the harvest, all the fields were open to be gleaned. Those who had the need and desire to glean simply went and worked wherever the inclination took them.

As Ruth takes up the role of gleaner, she finds herself reaping in a field belonging to Boaz. The term used in verse 3, "as it turned out", is full of deep spiritual meaning. Divine guidance was at work here. Ruth might not have realised it or sensed it, for most divine guidance takes place when we are unaware of it.

Most divine guidance takes place when we are unaware of it.

Father, forgive me for the times I have thought things have happened to me because of luck, when really it has been You. How glad I am that I am being guided not by the stars but by the Saviour. I am truly thankful. Amen.

UNDER HIS WINGS

For Reading and Meditation: Ruth 2:4–12

*May you be richly rewarded by the Lord ...
under whose wings you have come to take refuge." (v. 12)*

A s Boaz makes his way through the field, talking to his workers, his eye falls upon the figure of Ruth. "Who is she?" he asks. His workers quickly inform him that she is the widowed daughter-in-law of Naomi, a Moabite by birth.

We cannot be sure that it was love at first sight, but Boaz certainly shows all the signs of it. Listen to him as he walks over to Ruth and says: "Don't go and glean in another field and don't go away from here ... I have told the men not to touch you. And whenever you are thirsty, go and get a drink from the water jars the men have filled" (vv. 8–9). Now tell me, isn't that the language of a man in love? This protective care and concern prompts Ruth to ask: "Why have I found such favour in your eyes that you notice me – a foreigner?" (v. 10). Clearly, Boaz already knows of the return of Naomi and how her daughter-in-law Ruth has stayed at her side. He sums up his feelings in the words: "May the Lord repay you for what you have done. May you be richly rewarded by the Lord, the God of Israel, under whose wings you have come to take refuge" (v. 12).

I feel God wants me to tell many of you reading these lines that this is His special word to you today. Some of you have stood for Him despite great criticism from your families and friends. He has seen all your tears, all your heartache and all your sacrifices. And He promises you a perfect reward one day. Draw close to Him now and nestle beneath the shelter of His great wings. Look up and see how easily they cover you. Under His wings there is no further need for tears – just trust!

Under His wings there is no further need for tears – just trust!

O Father, how marvellous is Your timing. Just when I need it, You find a way of bringing me the greatest encouragement. When all other doors are closed, You find a secret stair into my soul. Thank You, dear Father. I take this word from You. Amen.

HANDFULS – ON PURPOSE

For Reading and Meditation: Ruth 2:13–17

"... pull out some stalks for her from the bundles and leave them for her to pick up ..." (v. 16)

We saw yesterday how Boaz, eager and anxious to keep Ruth in his field, sets about doing everything to ensure that her work as a gleaner is a free from problems as possible. Today we see how his protective concern leads him to invite Ruth to join him during a meal break. "Come over here," he says, "Have some bread and dip it in the wine vinegar" (v. 14). A little later he offers her some roasted grain. Gets more interesting doesn't it?

Once Ruth has completed her meal, she returns to her gleaning. Yet again, Boaz intervenes on her behalf by instructing his servants to let fall whole handfuls of grain so that she has plenty to gather. I love the way the Amplified Bible describes this moment: "And let fall some handfuls for her on purpose." "Handfuls ... on purpose." What a beautiful expression. It is a picture of how God goes before each one of His toiling servants and lets fall "handfuls on purpose" – some tokens of His goodness, some special encouragement, some evidence of His care, that serves to keep us moving forward and keep our hearts bent on the divine task.

Has there not been a time in your life when, overcome with the weight and burden of the day, you were about ready to give up the task God had given you, and suddenly He let fall some "handful on purpose"? Have you not experienced such a moment of divine encouragement? Perhaps it was a word in a sermon, a word from Scripture which was quickened by the Spirit in your heart, or perhaps a line in a devotional commentary. How gracious and loving is our Lord. Today He drops before you once again a "handful on purpose". Be glad for it.

God goes before each one of His toiling servants and lets fall "handfuls on purpose".

O Father, how easy it is to remember the discouragements and forget the encouragements. Forgive me for my proneness to do this. Thank You for every "handful on purpose" that comes my way. I bless You for them. In Jesus' Name.

ON LOOKING BACK

For Reading and Meditation: Ruth 2:18–21

"The Lord ... has not stopped showing his kindness to the living and the dead." (v. 20)

I t is not difficult to imagine the kind of thoughts that may have been going through Naomi's mind as she dwells on Ruth's first day in the harvest field. How will she fare? What will the men say about her – a foreigner? Will she be successful in bringing home enough grain to help keep body and soul together?

If Naomi had such fears then they are quickly laid to rest when Ruth returns to report on the events of the day with a whole ephah of barley. An ephah is no small measure. In today's terms it is about half a bushel, or nearly ten kilogrammes. Maybe this is my imagination overworking, but I can picture Ruth recounting the events of the day with great excitement – her whole being tingling with delight as she reflects on the way God has provided for her. Naomi's questions come fast and furious: "Tell me everything! Whose field were you in? Where did you glean?" As soon as Ruth mentions the name of Boaz, Naomi's heart leaps within her, and she begins to focus on the Lord in a way she has not quite done before. "The Lord bless him!" she says, referring of course to Boaz, "The Lord has not stopped showing his kindness to the living and the dead" (v. 20). Her joy knows no bounds because she senses that Ruth's meeting with Boaz has a providential feel about it. Boaz was a close relative who had the right to redeem Ruth and take her to be his wife.

Together, Ruth and Naomi look back over the day and give thanks to God for the evidence of His guiding hand. They find, as you and I have found, that the evidences of the divine design are certainly there as we look back.

Evidences of the divine design are certainly there as we look back.

Father, I confess I am better at looking back and thanking You than I am at looking ahead and praising You. Forgive me for that. Help me learn from what I have experienced of Your guiding hand to trust You more in the future. In Jesus' Name I pray. Amen.

IF ONLY WE BELIEVED

For Reading and Meditation: Ruth 2:22–23

"Ruth stayed close to the servant girls ... until the barley and wheat harvests were finished." (v. 23)

As the days and weeks of the barley harvest slip by, Ruth continues to glean in the field of Boaz, happy and secure in the knowledge that when the barley harvest is over she will be able to stay on and participate in the wheat harvest as well. Naomi is equally elated as she senses that Ruth's meeting with Boaz is no accident, but part of God's wonderful provision and care. One can imagine Naomi musing to herself: "How strange that Ruth should alight on the field owned by Boaz and that she should become the object of his personal interest and concern. And to discover, too, that Boaz has the right to redeem her and may well take her to be his wife." Deep down in her heart Naomi knows that God is at work.

And, with Naomi, each one of us must recognise that in the ebb and flow of life's circumstances, an eternal God is quietly pursuing His purposes. Little, if anything, happens by chance in the God-ordained life. The Almighty is seeking to work out His purposes in the life of each one of us, and He is there in every emergency or situation that arises. He is there in the ups and downs, the ins and outs, the comings and goings.

When you become aware of the fact that in the life of every one of His children God is bent on bringing to pass His perfect purposes, then although that thought does not entirely eliminate anxiety and fear, it most certainly reduces it. If only we could grasp the truth of Romans 8:28 (AV): "All things work together for good." I mean really grasp it. Hardly a fear would then arise in our hearts.

Our trouble is not that we do not believe God's Word; our trouble is we do not believe it enough.

> *Our trouble is not that we do not believe God's Word; our trouble is we do not believe it enough.*

My Father and my God, grant that Your Word might move from my intellect right into my heart. I don't want just to hold your Word; I want it to hold me. "I believe, help Thou mine unbelief." In Jesus' Name I ask it. Amen.

A BUDDING ROMANCE

For Reading and Meditation: Ruth 3:1–5

"Ruth ... went to the threshing-floor and did everything her mother-in-law told her to do." (v. 5)

As Naomi ponders the sovereignty of God in the meeting between Ruth and Boaz, she begins to realise there is a distinct possibility that Boaz will take on the responsibility of marrying Ruth and providing the security she needs in the future. She formulates a clear and daring plan to ensure the continuance of the budding romance. Note how she opens up the conversation: "My daughter, should I not try to find a home for you, where you will be well provided for? Is not Boaz ... a kinsman of ours?" (vv. 1–2).

During the time of the winnowing of the grain, it was customary for the workers to sleep on the threshing-floor. Naomi's first piece of advice to Ruth is this: "Wash and perfume yourself, and put on your best clothes" (v. 3).

It seems that in those days, just like today, men were attracted to well dressed and sweet smelling women! I am not sure that I know how to interpret her second piece of advice, however: "Don't let him know you are there until he has finished eating and drinking" (v. 3). Her third piece of advice is this: "When he lies down, note the place where he is lying. Then go and uncover his feet and lie down. He will tell you what to do" (v. 4). Naomi knew that according to the laws of Israel, a widow was entitled to approach the nearest male relative and remind him of his obligation to take care of her.

What a delightful picture this gives us of the relationship that exists between each one of us and our Lord Jesus Christ. Just as Ruth was within her legal rights in approaching Boaz, so we, as God's children, have a legal right to approach the throne of grace and avail ourselves of God's obligation to meet our every need.

> *We, as God's children, have a legal right to approach the throne of grace.*

Father, the thought that I have a legal right to approach Your throne and claim Your provision for my needs is awesome and breathtaking. Yet it is so. Help me to appropriate the rich inheritance I have in Christ. Amen.

A BINDING CONTRACT

For Reading and Meditation: Ruth 3:8–9

"Spread the corner of your garment over me, since you are a kinsman-redeemer." (v. 9)

We saw yesterday that Ruth, in approaching Boaz to remind him of his obligation to her under the law, was acting with perfect propriety and decorum. At midnight she moves in quietly to where Boaz is lying, gently uncovers his feet, and proceeds to lie across them. Boaz is somewhat startled by this act and enquires anxiously: "Who are you?" "I am your servant Ruth," she replies, "Spread the corner of your garment over me, since you are a kinsman-redeemer" (v. 9).

By this simple custom of lying at Boaz's feet Ruth was really saying: "I belong to you and I want you to take care of me." Boaz is seemingly thrilled to be approached in this way for his response is certain and positive: "The Lord bless you … don't be afraid. I will do for you all you ask" (vv. 10–11). We can safely assume from these words that at that moment he acceded to Ruth's request to cover her with his garment – the sign of his willingness to protect her and meet his obligations as a redeemer. The custom of covering a bride with a tallith, or fringed garment (Ezek. 16:8), is still part of Jewish matrimonial ritual to this day.

What spiritual lesson can be drawn from this beautiful and inspiring picture of Ruth lying at Boaz's feet? This – the Church, though surrounded at this present moment by a deep and dense darkness, is nevertheless resting safely and securely at the Saviour's feet. But this is not all. His covering of us by the robe of righteousness is also the pledge that one day He is going to join us to Himself in a marriage that will last for all eternity. And that marriage is destined never to end in divorce.

The Church is resting safely and securely at the Saviour's feet.

O Father, just to live with You in eternity would have been enough to delight my soul for ever, but to be joined to You, to be one with You, to be part of Your Bride, is more than I deserve. Yet that is Your promise. I am eternally grateful. Amen.

A "MOONLIGHT SONATA"

For Reading and Meditation: Ruth 3:10–13

"Although it is true that I am near of kin, there is a kinsman-redeemer nearer than I." (v. 12)

The more we get into the story of Ruth and Boaz, the more it appears that his heart was set on her right from the very start. He seems greatly relieved that she has approached him in this way, and the passage that occupies our attention today is a kind of "moonlight sonata" in which Boaz bears testimony to Ruth's virtue, courage, and character. It would appear from his statement that there was a little age difference between them. Listen again to what he says: "You have not run after the younger men, whether rich or poor" (v. 10). We cannot be certain about this, but most commentators make that deduction from these words.

One problem, however, faces the couple as they contemplate marriage. There is a closer relative than Boaz. Jewish law specifically required the next of kin, if he was single, to take on the responsibility of marrying a widow, but Boaz is second in line. He vows before the Lord that he will seek a settlement of the matter as quickly as possible, and then encourages Ruth to rest comfortably and contentedly until the morning.

Here we must ask ourselves the question: If there was a kinsman nearer than Boaz then why did not Ruth present herself to him? And why did not Naomi, who must have known there was a nearer kinsman than Boaz, steer Ruth in his direction? The answer will become clear as we reach the end of the story. For the moment, let it be enough to recognise in this the guiding and planning of the Almighty. The fate of most things precious is to grow familiar and lose their first bewildering thrill. May it never be so with the guidance of God.

Recognise the guiding and planning of the Almighty.

O Father, give me, I pray, an ever increasing consciousness of the wonder of divine guidance. Let the fact that "nothing is too trivial for Omnipotence" continually amaze and astonish me. In Jesus' Name I pray. Amen.

For Reading and Meditation: Ruth 3:14–18

"Bring me the shawl you are wearing ... he poured into it six measures of barley." (v. 15)

Boaz was well aware that Ruth's visit to him at midnight could be misinterpreted. Anxious to preserve her good name, he encourages her to return to her place before the rest of the workers awaken and the general activity of the day begins.

Before she leaves, however, he invites her to hold out her shawl, which he fills with six measures of barley. This was not something for which she had laboured, the result of her gleaning, but a special gift. One commentator describes it as "an engagement present", but there is no real evidence to see it in this light. In fact, a later comment by Ruth indicates that the gift was intended not only for her but for Naomi as well: "He gave me these six measures of barley, saying, 'Don't go back to your mother-in-law empty-handed' " (v. 17).

When Ruth finally reports to Naomi all that has happened in the night, and particularly the fact that there is a kinsman nearer than Boaz, Naomi gives her this advice: "Wait ... For the man will not rest until the matter is settled today" (v. 18). It is not easy to wait, especially where matters of the heart are concerned. But no Christian is mature until he or she has learned to wait.

Who can fail to see in these words a picture of Christ, our heavenly Boaz, who at the beginning of time set about the task of overcoming every obstacle that stood in the way of our salvation? Such was His commitment to us that He endured the most horrifying experiences to woo us, and win us to Himself.

No Christian is mature until he or she has learned to wait.

Gracious and loving Father, when I contemplated the tremendous obstacles and difficulties which my Lord Jesus Christ overcame to save me, there are just no words to express my gratitude and praise. Thank You, dear Father. Thank You. Amen.

THREE CONDITIONS

For Reading and Meditation: Ruth 4:1

*"When the kinsman-redeemer ... came along, Boaz
said, 'Come over here, my friend, and sit down.'" (v. 1)*

We have referred to the term "kinsman-redeemer"
several times in our meditations and we pause now to
make clear what it means.

The word "redeem", as you will know, means "to buy
back" or "set free". It is the act by which a person's property
or liberty is purchased through the payment of a special
price. A kinsman-redeemer was someone who became
involved in buying the rights and privileges of another
family member. As such, several things were required of
him. First, he must be a near kinsman, related by birth (Lev.
25:47–49). Second, he must be able to pay the required
price. Third, he must enter into any agreement willingly
and without coercion. All three of these conditions Boaz
was able to meet. He was related to Naomi by birth and was
thus a near kinsman. Being related to Naomi meant he was
also related to Ruth. It would appear he was well able to pay
the price, being a moderately wealthy land-owner. One
condition remains – was he willing? Most certainly so. So
great was his love for Ruth that he was willing to lay aside
his reputation in Israel and marry one who was cursed by
birth and frowned upon by Jewish law.

My mind flies, as I write, to another Kinsman-
Redeemer, whose name is Jesus. How wonderfully did our
Lord meet these three conditions. At the Incarnation He
joined Himself to us so that He could be classed as a
member of the human race and thus become a near
Kinsman. Although divested of heaven's riches, He had the
one thing needful to pay for our redemption – a perfect and
sinless life. And was He a willing participator? Again I say –
most certainly so.

*Another
Kinsman-
Redeemer,
whose
name is
Jesus.*

**Lord Jesus Christ, what a perfect Redeemer You are. You joined
Yourself to the human race in the Incarnation, paid for my
redemption with Your own life on the cross, and did all of this
freely and out of a heart of love. I am deeply thankful. Amen.**

A TEMPORARY SETBACK

For Reading and Meditation: Ruth 4:2–4

"'If you will redeem [the land], do so.' … 'I will redeem it,' he said." (v. 4)

What a day for celebration! Ruth, the Gentile widow from Moab, is to become the bride of the wealthy Boaz of Bethlehem. Before the marriage can take place, however, a special meeting has to be arranged with Naomi's next of kin so that the matter of redemption can be satisfactorily settled. The meeting is held at the gate of the city, the usual place for the elders to meet when resolving civic matters. Whatever was decided there usually became law. Boaz waits until the kinsman arrives and then proceeds to go into the details of Naomi's situation.

Here we are introduced to a new aspect of the story. It seems that Elimelech, Naomi's husband, had owned a field, and the first thing Boaz wants to do is to purchase that. The next of kin, however, has first claim and so Boaz asks the kinsman if he wants to buy it. For a moment it appears that Boaz's plan might be thwarted for the kinsman says: "I will buy it." If the nearest relative bought the dead man's land, Jewish law stated that he then had legal rights over the family. Should this happen now, Boaz would not be able to claim Ruth as his wife. Some might have turned away at this stage and said: "I have done all I can – there is nothing more I can do." But not Boaz. In his heart burned a love that would not be dampened by difficulties.

True love leaps over all obstacles.

This is the wonderful thing about true love – it leaps over all obstacles, opposes every argument, and moves on relentlessly until it possesses the object of its affection and makes it its own. Our Saviour's love was of this kind also – but of course infinitely greater. He has argued the case on our behalf and won! Now we find ourselves owned by Him – for ever.

O loving Saviour, how can I sufficiently thank You for pleading my case in the courts of heaven and winning on the cross my eternal freedom and redemption? What I feel is impossible to put into words. I love You Lord Jesus. Amen.

ARGUING THE CASE

For Reading and Meditation: Ruth 4:5–6

"… the kinsman-redeemer said '… I might endanger my own estate. You redeem it yourself.'" (v. 6)

We saw yesterday that Boaz's plans to redeem Ruth were temporarily thwarted when the nearest kinsman gave a definite "Yes" to his proposal that he should buy the land. But now watch as the love which burned in Boaz's heart gives energy to his thinking and he comes up with a powerful argument that wins the day.

Listen to that argument in the words of the Living Bible: "Then Boaz told him, 'Your purchase of the land from Naomi requires your marriage to Ruth so that she can have children to carry on her husband's name, and to inherit the land' " (v. 5). When presented with these facts, the kinsman's enthusiasm wanes. The thought of having a Moabitess in his family – one who was a despised alien – was not at all appealing, and so he says: "Then I can't do it ... For her son would become an heir to my property, too; you buy it" (v. 6).

How similar is all this to the process through which our Lord went in order to redeem us. Our Lord, too, was presented with a great problem as He set out to save us for, as Scripture puts it, we were "sold under sin" (Rom. 7:14, AV). That means we were slaves to the kingdom of Satan; we belonged by right to him. Christ, however, drawing on all His resources of infinite knowledge and wisdom, came up with a plan that enabled us to pass from the kingdom of Satan into the Kingdom of God. Satan thought he had us in his clutches for all time but he was out-manoeuvred at the cross. Just as Boaz turned the tables on the kinsman at Bethlehem, so our Lord turned the tables on Satan at Calvary. What the devil thought would be a great victory turned out to be his most ignominious defeat. Hallelujah!

Just as Boaz turned the tables on the kinsman at Bethlehem, so our Lord turned the tables on Satan at Calvary.

O Father, when I reflect on with what deftness and skill You overturned the strategies of Satan, I just want to open up my heart to You in endless praise. Blessed be Your Name for ever and ever. Amen.

THE REDEMPTION CEREMONY

For Reading and Meditation: Ruth 4:7–8

"... for the redemption ... to become final, one party took off his sandal and gave it to the other." (v. 7)

The ceremony through which a man passed when he was unwilling or unable to redeem something, and thus lost his legal claim, was both colourful and dramatic. This ceremony could, on occasions, be anything but pleasant. A widow, for example, who faced a hostile kinsman who did not want to fulfil his obligations under the law, would sometimes spit in his face and say: "This is what is done to the man who will not build up his brother's family line" (Deut. 25:9).

The law required that the man who was transferring his legal right should take off his shoe and hand it to the other person as an act of sealing – the transaction was now complete. Another requirement of the law, when a transaction such as this took place, was that it should be done in the full view of the public. Justice must not only be done but be seen to be done.

Once again, how reminiscent this is of the work of Christ on the cross of Calvary. Paul says when speaking of our redemption: "This thing was not done in a corner" (Acts 26:26, AV). He meant by this that our Lord was not put to death in one of the back streets of Jerusalem, away from the eyes of the multitudes, but was crucified on a hill for all to see. There was a divine purpose behind this. If Christ had died at the hand of a footpad in some quiet corner of the city then His death would have exposed the evil of only one man – a criminal type of individual. The fact that Christ was officially put to death – the "best" people of the nation sought it – meant that their condemnation of Him was representative of the wishes of the whole human race. In the uplifted cross we have a revelation of the real character of humanity.

Justice must not only be done but be seen to be done.

Father, I see that the cross exposes not just the sins of a few but the sins of all humanity. This means my sins are there also. But man did not take Your life away from You; You laid it down of Yourself. I am so grateful for this saving truth. Amen.

SEALED AND CERTIFIED

For Reading and Meditation: Ruth 4:9–12

"Then Boaz announced to the elders and all the people, 'Today you are witnesses ...'" (v. 9)

Consider how Boaz places such emphasis on the transaction between him and the nearest kinsman being made before witnesses. He begins and ends his statement with these words: "Today you are witnesses." Why this double emphasis? I suggest it was because Boaz wanted to be sure that the transaction would never be called into question. It wasn't every day that a Jew married a Gentile, especially a Moabitess. People might query the legality of this in the future if not now clearly sealed, settled and certified.

After Boaz has declared to the witnesses that he accepts the full responsibility of kinsman-redeemer to Naomi which meant Ruth becoming his wife, the elders respond by reciting the traditional blessing: "May the Lord make the woman who is coming into your home like Rachel and Leah" (v. 11). If the elders had had any doubts about Boaz marrying a Moabitess, then clearly those doubts had all been removed. Their wish for Ruth is that she will be as blessed as Rachel and Leah, the two wives of Jacob, whose names were used in the Bible as a byword for fruitfulness. Rachel was regarded by Israel as one of their most illustrious personages. It seems most strange that the elders should wish for Ruth to become as honoured and revered as Rachel, especially when we remember that Ruth was from a land under God's curse. What produced this strange turn of events? Just one simple factor – Boaz. By marrying Ruth, he brought about a change in her identity and this, of course, was recognized by all.

Christ has joined Himself to us and given us His own identity.

This is precisely what Christ has done for us. Though we were classified as "children of wrath" and "excluded from citizenship in Israel and foreigners to the covenants of promise" (Eph. 2:3, AV; 2:12), Christ has joined Himself to us and given us His own identity. We are no longer aliens – we belong to Him.

O God, how can I ever praise You enough for plucking me out of the world and giving me a new heart, a new identity, and one day a new name? Eternal praise and glory be unto Your precious Name. Amen.

A PLACE IN HISTORY

For Reading and Meditation: Ruth 4:11–12

"May you have standing in Ephrathah and be famous in Bethlehem." (v. 11)

We continue meditating on the words of blessing given by the elders at the completion of the legal formalities entered into by Boaz: "May the Lord make the woman who is coming into your home like Rachel and Leah" (v. 11). To see the real significance of these words, we have to jump ahead a little and consider come of the events that took place subsequent to the marriage of Ruth and Boaz.

In due course, a son was born whose name was Obed. When Obed grew up and reached maturity, he then married and had a son named Jesse. From Jesse came David, one of the greatest of all Bible characters. When we trace the line of Ruth down through the centuries, we come to the passage we looked at during the opening days of our meditations – Matthew 1 – where we saw the name of Ruth listed alongside the others who were part of our Lord's genealogy. Ruth's name, being included in our Lord's line of descent, is stamped with a dignity that even Rachel never had!

Consider what else the elders said as they gave Boaz and Ruth their blessing: "May you have standing in Ephrathah [the area surrounding the city of David] and be famous in Bethlehem" (v. 11). Bethlehem has a cherished place in history for two main reasons. One, it is the city of David, and two, it is the birthplace of our Lord Jesus Christ. It is impossible to think of Bethlehem without thinking of King David. And the great-grandmother of David was Ruth. The blessing given by the elders turned out to be more than a blessing; it was a prophecy. Ruth has become as well known in Israel as Rachel and Leah, and her standing is as solid and immovable as that of the city of Bethlehem.

Ruth has become as well known in Israel as Rachel and Leah.

Father, the more I follow the story of Ruth, the more convinced I am that Your sovereign purposes are at work even when nothing seems to go right. Deepen this conviction in me hour by hour and day by day. In Jesus' Name. Amen.

REFLECTED GLORY

For Reading and Meditation: Ruth 4:13

"So Boaz took Ruth and she became his wife." (v. 13)

W e come now to the moment we have all been waiting for – the hour when Boaz takes Ruth to be his wife. I must confess to a slight sense of anticlimax as I read the account of their marriage, for all the Bible says is this: "So Boaz took Ruth and she became his wife." How I wish the inspired writer of the book of Ruth had included a few more details about the wedding. I would like to know what she wore. What did Naomi say as she watched her beloved daughter-in-law being joined in matrimony to Boaz? We have to recognise, of course, that had God wished us to know these details, they would have been recorded, and so we must be content with things the way they are.

What intrigues me, however, is that immediately prior to the marriage, Ruth seems to be very much in the background. There is a reason for this, I believe, in keeping with the message of the book. It is, after all, the story of a Moabitess, a penniless widow, over whom hung a curse, finding favour and salvation through the intervention of another. The law of Israel barred Ruth's way to happiness and prosperity until grace made itself known in the form of Boaz.

Law knows no mercy; it demands only justice. Grace, however, looks for a way to satisfy the law's demands and bring happiness and joy to the guilty. Like Ruth, we had no legal claim to God's blessings. However, because Christ, the heavenly Boaz, has entered our lives, cleared all our debt, and made Himself responsible for our eternal future, we are content to seek no glory for ourselves but to ascribe it all to Him. Any glory we receive is a reflected glory; it comes to us from Him.

Any glory we receive is a reflected glory.

O Father, that I should receive any glory at all – even a reflected glory – is beyond my comprehension. Yet I know it is to be. All I can say is that the glory You give to me, I will give back to You. Thank You my Father. Amen.

WEDDING IN THE SKIES

For Reading and Meditation: Ruth 4:13–17

"The women living there said, 'Naomi has a son.'
And they named him Obed." (v. 17)

The last few verses of the book of Ruth inform us of the birth of Obed, and tell how Naomi cares for the child as Ruth and Boaz continue a normal family life in the agricultural setting of Bethlehem.

As we have already referred to the birth of Obed, the question I want to consider now is this: Where was Ruth while the arrangements to redeem her were being made? She was waiting patiently in the house of her mother-in-law, Naomi. Remember Naomi's words: "Wait ... until you find out what happens" (3:18)? We have no reason to suppose that Ruth waited with anything other than absolute confidence in the ability of Boaz to accomplish what he promised.

Now let me pose another question: Where is our Saviour at this present moment? Yes, of course – in heaven. And what is He doing there? Many things, but one thing in particular – He is attending to the arrangements for the wedding which is one day to take place between Himself and His Church. While this is being done, we, the bride of Christ here on earth, are expected to wait patiently for the day when He will come to receive us to Himself. Just as Ruth waited patiently to hear the voice of the maidens who, as was the custom, came to accompany the bride to her wedding, crying out "Behold the Bridegroom cometh", so we too wait for that same cry that will herald the return of our Lord. We are going to a wedding in the skies which, by the way, is not called the wedding of the Church, but the wedding of the Lamb (Rev. 19:7). And why? Because, as the old hymn so beautifully puts it: "The Lamb is all the glory, in Immanuel's land."

We are going to a wedding in the skies.

Lord Jesus Christ, help me wait for Your coming down here on earth as You wait for it in heaven. Help me remember that the only reason You delay Your coming is that more might be gathered in. I wait with patience – but also with eager anticipation. Amen.

FROM A MESS – A MESSAGE

For Reading and Meditation: Ruth 4:18–22

"Obed the father of Jesse, and Jesse the father of David." (v. 22)

We come now to the last day of our Meditations in the book of Ruth and we reflect together on the main theme and message of this delightful story. What is the book of Ruth really saying to us? This – through all the mistakes, blunders, heartaches, problems and difficulties of life, God is continually at work, guiding, governing, and controlling all our days.

We have seen this thrilling truth illustrated in the life of the little family who, after leaving Bethlehem during a time of famine, made their way to Moab where they met with tragedy and disappointment. When, at last, Naomi, the only survivor from that original family returns to Bethlehem in company with her daughter-in-law, Ruth, it is to discover that God is able to bring joy out of sorrow, delight out of disappointment and good out of evil. "Many things," said Thomas Erskine, "appear irretrievable to us, but there is nothing irretrievable with God."

So learn to drop your anchor into the depths of this reassuring and encouraging revelation – out of every mess God is able to make a message. Never forget that the God and Father of Ruth, Boaz and Naomi, is also the God and Father of our Lord Jesus Christ, and through our Kinsman-Redeemer has become our God as well. In heaven He is preparing for us a new home where we will abide with Him for ever. Surely the four short chapters we have studied together over these past weeks reveal so much to us of the goodness and sovereignty of God that our lives cannot help but be enriched. God's way is always best; take it and you will obtain its rewards. Take another way, your own way, and all you will get are consequences.

> *"Many things appear irretrievable to us, but there is nothing irretrievable with God."*

Father, thank You for showing me in such detail the truth that You have the power and ability to turn a tragedy into a triumph. Help me keep the truths I have learned ever before me. In Jesus' Name I ask it. Amen.

LIVING DANGEROUSLY

For Reading and Meditation: Esther 4:10–17

"And who knows but that you have come to royal position for such a time as this?" (v. 14)

W e turn now to examine together the only other book of the Bible which is named after a woman – the book of Esther. You are probably familiar with the fact that this is the only book of the Bible which does not actually mention the name of God. But it has to be pointed out that although His name is not to be seen, the evidences of His guiding and controlling hand are everywhere.

Before actually beginning to study the book section by section, I want to use these first two days to acquaint you with one or two of its high points – hence today's reading. The verse I have chosen is without doubt the highlight of the book and introduces us to its main message and theme – the sovereignty of God at work in the lives of His people. In a way, this theme is similar to the one which we have just studied, and I make no apology for exposing you yet again to this subject. Unless we hold in our hearts the solid conviction that God is on the throne, our lives will soon become drained of all point and purpose. The Christian who says, "I am not sure whether God is at work in my life or not," is living dangerously. The way we think greatly influences the way we feel, and if our perception of things is that they are haphazard and without point and purpose then we will finish up, as someone put it, "with loud days that have no meaning and no end".

As we peruse the pages of Esther together, I trust you will come, as countless thousands of others down the running ages have come, to experience not merely a faith that you hold but a faith that holds you.

Experience not merely a faith that you hold but a faith that holds you.

Father, I realise that when I live out my days here on earth with no clear understanding of Your overall direction and control, I live dangerously. Open up once again the truth of Your divine sovereignty to my understanding. In Jesus' Name. Amen.

A FIXED POINT

For Reading and Meditation: Esther 7:1–10

"So they hanged Haman on the gallows he had prepared for Mordecai." (v. 10)

We look now at the second highlight of the book of Esther – the downfall and defeat of the scheming Haman. This verse, and the one we looked at yesterday, form the two hinges on which the book turns. One shows us the sovereignty of God in placing Esther in the king's palace during a time of impending peril, and the other points to the ultimate end of evil.

I want to spend today underlining once more the need for each one of us to hold in our hearts the solid conviction that God is on the throne, and no matter how things appear, it is His purposes that eventually hold sway. Many years ago, I studied the book of Esther during a time of great spiritual drought, and I caught such a vision of God's sovereignty and power that it turned my life around. I long that the same thing might happen to you.

Let me be absolutely frank with you. We are in a storm. The people of God are being subjected to extreme pressure not only from Satan but also from an increasingly hostile world. If we are to keep our sanity in a world that is seemingly going mad then we must be sure that we have some concrete convictions to guide us through the days. Opinions are not enough. Just as a mariner has to be sure of the utter dependability of the points from which he takes his bearings, so we too must be sure of certain elemental dogmas as we make our way through the world. A conviction concerning God's sovereignty is one of them. The book of Esther is one of those fixed points from which we are able to take our spiritual bearings. An understanding of the book will enable us to avoid the spiritual shipwreck that many seem to be making of their lives in today's world.

> *No matter how things appear, it is God's purposes that eventually hold sway.*

My Father and my God, I am on a difficult journey through life but I am thankful that You have charted my course with care. I have fixed points from which to take my bearings – the book of Esther being one of them. I am so very grateful. Amen.

WORLD FAIR – 482 BC

For Reading and Meditation: Esther 1:1–8

"... in the third year of his reign he gave a banquet for all his nobles and officials." (v. 3)

Before we begin our journey verse by verse through the book of Esther, we pause to note that this book is one of the two books of the Old Testament in which an orthodox Jew is required to make any solemn oath or vow – the other being the Pentateuch, the books of Moses. The reason for this is that Moses recounts the deliverance of the Jews from Egypt, and the book of Esther recounts the deliverance of the Jews from what could have been one of the greatest massacres of all time.

The opening verses of Esther introduce us to a sensual and capricious king called Xerxes (known in Hebrew as Ahasuerus). One day he decided to put on a great pageant for his lords and ladies – a kind of World Fair. The planning of this great celebration took six months and culminated with a magnificent banquet (v. 6). Despite the monarch's sensuality, however, he stipulated that no one had to drink unless he wanted to (v. 8). In doing this, he showed much more sense than many in today's world who frown on those who don't drink, regarding them as "kill joys" or unsociable.

The debate concerning whether the Bible teaches teetotalism has gone on for centuries. But whether or not it does, Christians ought to be very cautious about the use of alcohol. Such is the pressure of living in today's world that many turn to drink as a pick-me-up. A doctor told me that quite a number of his Christian patients were on the verge of alcoholism. It might be a good idea if, before going any farther, we were to take a look at where our daily support comes from – alcoholic spirit or the Holy Spirit. What need have we for crutches when we can be held by the ever-lasting arms?

What need have we for crutches when we can be held by the everlasting arms?

Gracious and loving Father, forgive me if I am more dependent on the things that affect my senses than on You, the living God. I come afresh to You today for cleansing, forgiveness and dedication. Help me, my Father. In Jesus' Name. Amen.

WIFELY SUBMISSION

For Reading and Meditation: Esther 1:10–12

"But when the attendants delivered the king's command, Queen Vashti refused to come." (v. 12)

The next person we meet in the kingdom of Xerxes is his wife, Vashti, the queen. We know very little about Vashti except that she was, to all appearances, a sensible, respectable and very beautiful woman. On the seventh day of the great banquet, King Xerxes, heavily under the influence of alcohol, directs his chamberlains to go and get Vashti that he might display her beauty to the guests. On the surface, this appears a harmless request, but some commentators believe what he was really wanting her to do was to disrobe in front of his guests. If this was so, then it would explain why she refused to obey the king's command.

Although the Bible commands a wife to submit to her husband (Eph. 5:22), such obedience is not to be seen as unconditional. If a man orders his wife to do something lewd, dishonest, or immoral, then she has every right to refuse to submit to such a command. Those who teach the submission of a wife to her husband often overlook this point. God does not require a wife to submit to her husband when he wants her to do something that goes against Scripture.

But the matter must not be left there. Any woman faced with a command from her husband to do something wrong, improper and unscriptural ought to ask God for wisdom to come up with a creative alternative. Remember what Daniel did when asked to violate Scripture? He came up with a creative alternative that went some way to meeting the king's desires but did not compromise his convictions (Dan. 1:8–16). Many a wife could be saved from being intimidated spiritually by remembering this.

God does not require a wife to submit to her husband when he wants her to do something that goes against Scripture.

Heavenly Father, I see that although submission to authority is a clear Biblical principle, I am never expected to obey a command that violates Your Word. But whenever it is necessary to disobey, help me to do so wisely, creatively and in love. Amen.

LOVING LEADERSHIP

For Reading and Meditation: Esther 1:13–22

"... the queen's conduct will become known to all the women, and so they will despise their husbands ..." (v. 17)

Vashti's refusal to obey the king's command threw the whole palace into an uproar. The Persian regime was established and built on the concept of law and order. So deeply ingrained was this idea that even the king himself was subject to the laws that he signed.

Greatly embarrassed by Vashti's behaviour, he turns to his chamberlains for advice. They were upset, too, not so much out of concern for the king but because Vashti's action might spark off a women's liberation movement that would spread throughout the whole of the empire. They decide to nip the whole matter in the bud, and recommend to the king that Vashti be removed from office and her place filled with someone more co-operative and submissive. In addition, they suggest that the king make a decree commanding every wife in the land to honour her husband "from the least to the greatest" (v. 20).

Some Christian husbands adopt a similar attitude in their marriages. They say: "I am the head and that means I must be obeyed at all costs. God has made this decree in His Word and I am here to enforce it." It is perfectly true that God gives spiritual headship to the man in marriage, but that headship is to be operated under the law of love. A man is to love his wife and lead her "as Christ loved the church" (Eph. 5:25). And how does Christ lead and love the Church? With great tenderness and sensitivity. Any man who adopts the position of "I'm the boss so you had better obey" is not following the leadership example of Christ. He is not a leader; he is a dictator. And such an attitude is alien to the Spirit of Christ.

And how does Christ lead and love the Church? With great tenderness and sensitivity.

Father, I know that it takes great skill to handle a relationship, especially that of marriage. Help me to bring the attitude of Jesus into all my relationships. In Jesus' Name I ask it. Amen.

ENTER MORDECAI

For Reading and Meditation: Esther 2:1-6

*"Now there was in the citadel of Susa a Jew
of the tribe of Benjamin." (v. 5)*

Having taken steps to remove Vashti from the throne, plans are set in motion for the selection of a new queen. Thus the first "Miss World" contest gets under way. The king appoints officers in all the provinces of his kingdom, presumably to arrange knock-out competitions so that by process of elimination only the best candidates would appear before him.

At this point a third person appears in our story – Mordecai the Jew. We read: "Now there was in the citadel of Susa a Jew." This is the first time the word "Jew" is mentioned in the book, but is a word, as we shall see, that appears over and over again, albeit derogatively.

Mordecai's great-grandfather had been taken into captivity in Babylon over a hundred years before, in the days of Nebuchadnezzar, in company with such famous names as Daniel and Ezekiel. About sixty years before the events recorded in Esther, in 539 BC, Cyrus the Persian conquered Babylon. He issued a decree allowing the Jews to return to Jerusalem to rebuild the Temple, destroyed by Nebuchadnezzar. Many exiles returned to Jerusalem, but others preferred to stay in Babylon or move to other parts of the Persian empire. For some reason, Mordecai settled in Susa, one of the Persian capitals. I say "for some reason", but really it was a divine reason. It was so that he might be the right man in the right place at the right time.

We saw something of the way in which God guides His people in the story of Ruth – and here we see it again. How marvellous is the wisdom of God who sees the end from the beginning.

How marvellous is the wisdom of God who sees the end from the beginning.

O Father, forgive me that I am so slow to recognise Your guiding and governing hand in my life. Make me alert and sensitive to the fact that I am being guided, even when I am not conscious of it. In Jesus' Name. Amen.

"BEAUTIFUL AND LOVELY"

For Reading and Meditation: Esther 2:7–8

"… the maiden was beautiful and lovely …" (v. 7, RSV)

Yesterday we saw how God's purposeful and loving hand had gently guided Mordecai to Susa in Persia in order that he might be the right man in the right place at the right time. Today we meet the woman who is the centre-piece of the story – the lovely Esther. She was, in fact, the adopted daughter of Mordecai. He had taken her into his personal care following the death of her mother and father some years previously.

It is surely significant that we are introduced to Esther with these words: "The maiden was beautiful and lovely" (v. 7, RSV). Why significant? Because these words imply she was a woman fit to be a queen. Mordecai, being aware of the contest to find a suitable queen for King Xerxes, decides to put forward Esther's name as a contender for the title. Such a decision appears on the face of it to be completely opposed to everything Mordecai believed as a Jew. Most Jews in that period of time regarded a mixed marriage as something to be strictly avoided. But that apart, what man in his right mind would want his daughter married to as sensual and capricious a person as Xerxes? No doubt he considered these factors, but something urged him to enter Esther in the contest.

This is what we mean when we talk about the sovereignty of God. It makes itself known in many different ways, one being the gentle pressure that the Almighty places on a person's mind, urging him to do or say something that might be against his natural inclinations. And however difficult that is to understand, one discovers that God's leadings always turn out right.

God's leadings always turn out right.

O Father, where would I be today were it not for Your sovereign purposes quietly being worked out in my life? How grateful I am for the gentle pressure of Your Holy Spirit that turns me from one path to another. All honour and glory be to Your wonderful Name. Amen.

WHEN PLANS ARE CROSSED

For Reading and Meditation: Esther 2:8–9

"The girl pleased him and won his favour." (v. 9)

One of the most fascinating things about Old Testament history is the way in which God used those who did not believe Him to further His purposes. Cyrus, the creator of the Persian empire, is one such example. Yet Isaiah shows us how, behind all his conquests, a divine purpose was at work: "I will strengthen you, though you have not acknowledged me" (Isa. 45:5).

We see a similar pattern in the passage before us today. Esther, having been brought to the palace as one of the finalists, finds herself before Hegai, the contest co-ordinator. Our text tells us: "The girl pleased him and won his favour." This was not the first time God had given one of His ambassadors favour with a king's representative. It happened also to Joseph (Gen. 41:9–14). And just as Joseph was a divine instrument to the people of his day, so was Esther to her people. Unknown to anyone in the royal palace, God was setting the stage for the deliverance of His people.

We begin to see now even more clearly why Mordecai and Esther were in the royal city of Susa, and not in Jerusalem, the capital of their own land, where the walls still lay in ruins and the comparatively small numbers of Jews who had returned from exile in Babylon were dispirited. There they could have served a useful purpose, but they became part of a greater and wiser plan – to save the Jews from extinction in Persia.

Remember, the next time your personal plans are over-turned – God allows our own plans to be broken so that we, with Him, can build bigger and better ones.

God allows our own plans to be broken so that we, with Him, can build bigger and better ones.

Gracious and loving heavenly Father, may I ever be open to the possibility that in the thwarting of my plans, greater and wiser purposes are being worked out. And help me receive the thwarting of my plans not with resignation but with rejoicing. Amen.

GOD'S PATIENCE

For Reading and Meditation: Esther 2:10–14

"Esther had not revealed her nationality ... because Mordecai had forbidden her to do so." (v. 10)

The advice given by Mordecai to Esther that under no circumstance is she to reveal she is a Jewess indicates that he had some awareness of God's purpose to use Esther's presence in the palace to accomplish divine ends.

No doubt the Jews were as hated in Persia as they were in Nazi Germany in World War II. What accounts for this phenomenon which we call anti-Semitism? Some say it arises because of the Jewish preoccupation with making money. Others say it is part of God's judgment upon them for their repeated acts of rebellion against Him in the past. Some explain it in terms of xenophobia – the fear of strangers. The real reason, I think, is quite simply because the Jews are God's chosen people. Not His only people, but a people chosen to display a special purpose. They clearly have that stamp upon them.

We read that every day Mordecai appeared at the gate of the palace in order to learn how Esther was doing. Tactfully, he enquired day after day about her condition and her progress. There must have been many times when he thought to himself: How long can she keep her Jewish identity a secret? Will she, by some innocent remark, somehow let it slip? Mordecai's daily vigil went on not for a period of a few weeks, but for twelve months! This a long time to await the outcome of any decision, and it says a good deal about the patience and persistence of Mordecai, who was undoubtedly sustained by the knowledge that God was quietly working out His perfect purposes.

God was quietly working out His perfect purposes.

Heavenly Father, forgive me for my impatience with Your patience. Help me understand that with You things never get off course. You may be slow, but You are always sure. May I never lose my grip on that fact. In Jesus' Name I pray. Amen.

CHOSEN AS QUEEN

For Reading and Meditation: Esther 2:15–20

*"Now the king was attracted to Esther more
than to any of the other women ..." (v. 17)*

The twelve-month period for those who were being
groomed for selection as queen is now at an end and the
day arrives on which the new queen of Persia is to be
selected.

Esther, along with the other contestants, is given access
to all the perfume and finery that she desires. Just imagine
that! It's rather like a husband letting his wife loose in the
famous Harrods store in Knightsbridge, London, and saying:
"Whatever you need to look your best – get it. It's all
yours!" Esther selects what she desires and then, suitably
dressed, is presented to the king. Xerxes takes one look at
the beautiful Esther and loses his heart to her right away.
There is absolutely no doubt in his mind; this is the woman
he wants to be his wife. Esther is to be the new queen of
the land, and all this takes place without her Jewish identity being made known. So far so good! Quietly and
unhurriedly, God has brought about the first stage in His
plans to protect and deliver His people.

The selection of Esther as queen is probably one of the
most important moments in the calendar of God. To gaze
on this scene and not to thrill at the marvellous workings of
the divine mind would be strange indeed. We must use it to
reinforce the conviction that ought to be in the heart of
every Christian, namely the fact that God never vacates His
throne. Let me assure you once again that even though
there may be times when God appears to have no interest in
the march of the moments, He is working out His purposes
nevertheless. Only blind ignorance interprets His silence as
weakness. As a poet once put it – history is His story!

*God never
vacates His
throne.*

**O Father, drive this powerful and important truth more deeply
into my spirit than it has ever been before. Fashion it into the
shape of an anchor that will hold me steady in the fiercest of
storms. This I ask in Jesus' precious and peerless Name. Amen.**

For Reading and Meditation: Esther 2:21–3:4

"Mordecai found out about the plot and told Queen Esther, who ... reported it to the king ..." (v. 22)

Now that God has successfully brought Esther into favour with the king, His purpose is to do exactly the same for Mordecai.

One day, as Mordecai sits outside the palace, he happens to overhear two palace guards plotting to assassinate the king. Ordinarily, Mordecai would have been unable to convey this news to the palace. The matter was deadly serious as the guards, being keepers of the palace doors, had not only motive but opportunity. There was no time to be lost if the king's life was to be saved. Mordecai quickly passes a message to Esther who, in turn, informs the king of the situation. An immediate investigation is made, the guards are interrogated, and once their guilt is established they are hanged. After the hanging, a record is made of the whole episode, right down to the name of Mordecai who had first informed about the matter. That record, as we shall see, was also to play a strategic part in the bringing about of God's purposes.

In his position as second-in-command to the king, Haman received from the community a good deal of respect and obedience. Whenever he appeared in public, people would bow before him, but there was one man who refused to do this – Mordecai. As a Jew, he should bow to no one but Jehovah. Mordecai's friends, fearing for his safety, tried to persuade him in every way they could but Mordecai was adamant – he would bow only to the Creator and not to a creature. Perhaps his friends argued that he ought to sacrifice principle for policy and thus live on to pursue his cause. Mordecai, however, refused to listen to the voice of expediency, believing it right to honour God no matter what the consequences.

Bow only to the Creator and not to a creature.

Father, help me to remember that doing the right thing is always the right thing to do. Make me a person or principle so that my policies have something to keep them on course. In Jesus' Name I ask it. Amen.

A DIABOLICAL PLAN

For Reading and Meditation: Esther 3:5–8

"Yet having learned who Mordecai's people were,
he scorned the idea of killing only Mordecai." (v. 6)

When the news is carried to Haman that one man in the kingdom will not bow down to him, he is extremely angry. By this time it is a well known fact that Mordecai is a Jew. Haman, bearing as he did a strong hatred of the Jewish people, would have liked to have ended Mordecai's life there and then. He knows, however, that to act in this way would not endear him to the people for there was in Persia at that time a great respect for the processes of the law. Also, people might have said: "What kind of fear must exist in Haman's heart if he is afraid of one solitary Jew?"

Haman begins to think up a plan that will bring him the revenge he seeks and a fiendish idea crosses his mind – why not exterminate the whole of the Jewish race? History is replete with instances of people who have tried to exterminate the Jews. Behind these plans and ideas lies the arch-enemy of the human race himself – Satan.

The devil knows there are two classes of people who are specially chosen by God in the world – the Jewish nation and the Church of God. And his hatred, as history shows, is aimed at both. If Satan had been able to exterminate the Jews then there would have been no Redeemer and no Saviour, for it was prophesied that our Lord would be of Jewish descent. Strange though it may seem, it is Satan's hatred of the Jews that has kept the race alive through every century. Their persecution served, in turn, to keep them together and developed in them a strong and powerful desire to maintain their identity no matter what. Another evidence of how God uses adverse circumstances as "grist to His mill".

God uses adverse circumstances as "grist to His mill".

My Father and my God, the more I see how nothing can frustrate Your eternal purposes, the more I realise how unnecessary are my fears. Let these truths that I am considering permeate every part of my soul. In Jesus' Name I pray. Amen.

A MISMATCHED CONTEST

For Reading and Meditation: Esther 3:9–15

"If it pleases the king, let a decree be issued to destroy them …" (v. 9)

Clearly, Haman knew that his plan to exterminate the Jews needed careful thought and delicate handling if it was to succeed. As Persia prided itself on its structure of law, his first task was to draw up a new edict which demanded the death of all those who were Jews, then have it approved by the king.

When, at last, the cruel document is finished, it is brought to the king who apparently without question signs it, and by so doing establishes it as a new law. The document, of course, was full of lies, which is not surprising when you consider that behind it was the one of whom Jesus once referred to as "the father of lies" – the devil (John 8:44). Haman's hatred and malevolence towards the Jews was so great that he offered to finance the whole cost of the operation to exterminate them himself. The amount, we are told, was 10,000 talents of silver, an amount in modern currency of about twenty-five million pounds, or forty-five million dollars. Doubtless, Haman considered this to be an investment, believing that his financial outlay would be returned to him later in the form of repossessed Jewish property and treasures. Once the decree was signed and sealed, it was translated into the many languages of the subject peoples and sent to every part of the empire. The edict said that on the 13th day of a certain month, every Jew would be put to death. No one would be exempt. It demanded complete extermination.

Haman was to find out, however, what other leaders of nations throughout time have found – that those who set out to exterminate the Jews are fighting against God. And what a mismatched contest that always turns out to be!

Those who set out to exterminate the Jews are fighting against God.

Gracious and loving heavenly Father, how glad I am that I am not fighting against You, but fighting for You. As I fight this "good fight of faith", help me understand that with You on my side I may lose a few rounds but never the contest. I am so thankful. Amen.

ALWAYS AHEAD!

For Reading and Meditation: Esther 4:1–9

"Hathach went back and reported to Esther what Mordecai had said." (v. 9)

When the news of Haman's cruel edict reaches the ears of Mordecai, his reaction is one of stunned sorrow. He realises that because of his unwillingness to bow before Haman, now every Jewish man, woman and child is to be annihilated.

Immediately, he casts off his clothes and puts on sackcloth and ashes – the accepted Jewish symbol of deep mourning. Dressed in this way, Mordecai makes his way to the palace gates in the hope that someone inside might see him and inform Esther of his condition. His plan works, and as soon as news is passed to Esther about his unusual appearance, she wonders as to the cause. She has not yet heard about Haman's plan to kill all Jews and thus she can only speculate about the reason for his strange behaviour. She asks herself: What kind of trouble can Mordecai be in? Loss of property or money perhaps? Dispatching a messenger to the palace gates with a fresh supply of clothing and instructions to find out what is causing Mordecai such deep sorrow, she learns for the first time of Haman's plan to exterminate her people.

Perhaps it was at this moment that Mordecai and Esther began to gain some insight into the purpose of their being in the royal city of Susa in Persia. Sometimes we fail to recognise the guidance of God until we are face to face with a crisis. Then how reassuring it is to know that the God who has foreseen everything, and has gone before us, is unfailingly at work to bring all things to a positive end. I was taught in Sunday school a song that went like this: "He who has led, will lead." Now, it is more than a song; it is a constant spiritual support.

"He who has led, will lead."

O God, forgive me that I so easily forget You are not only around me, beneath me, and above me, but also ahead of me. Nothing can happen to me that You have not foreseen or anticipated. May this truth be also my constant support. In Jesus' Name. Amen.

"YOU HAVE A DESTINY"

For Reading and Meditation: Esther 4:10–14

"And who knows but that you have come to royal position for such a time as this?" (v. 14)

When Esther receives the message from Mordecai requesting her to meet urgently with the king and plead with him to repeal the edict authorising the massacre of her people, she is at a loss to know how to proceed. Listen to her response, this time from the Living Bible: "All the world knows that anyone, whether man or woman, who goes into the king's inner court without his summons is doomed to die unless the king holds out his golden sceptre; and the king has not called for me to come to him in more than a month." To which Mordecai replies in words that have become a spiritual classic: "If you keep quiet at a time like this, God will deliver the Jews from some other source, but you and your relatives will die; what's more, who can say but that God has brought you into the palace for just such a time as this?" (vv. 11, 14). The appeal was perfect. It was the motivation Esther needed and her spirit is quickened by the thought that God, in His perfect purposes, has prepared her for this very moment.

I believe that these are the words which God wants to come alive in your own life today. You too are a person of destiny, and have come into God's kingdom for such a time as this. A preacher tells how his young daughter came home from a Christian youth camp and said excitedly: "Dad, they told me at camp I have a destiny." Then about an hour or two later she said: "Dad, what's a destiny?" She had one but didn't quite know what it was. Many Christians are like that. They are here for a purpose but they don't know what it is. God has destined you to do something particular, and if you don't do it, then it just won't get done. My destiny is to write *Every Day with Jesus*. What's yours?

You too are a person of destiny, and have come into God's kingdom for such a time as this.

O Father, can it really be true that You have put me in Your kingdom to fulfil a purpose that is solely mine? I must believe it. Show me my destiny, dear Lord. Make it crystal clear to me I pray. In Jesus' Name. Amen.

TIME TO FAST

For Reading and Meditation: Esther 4:15–17

"Go, gather together all the Jews who are in Susa, and fast for me." (v. 15)

Mordecai's appeal to Esther that she should look at the situation in the light of God's sovereignty convinces her that she should get to see the king as quickly as possible. As so much is at stake, she wisely decides to enter into a three-day fast and, informing Mordecai of her decision, she requests him to join her in this spiritual discipline. She suggests, also, that he urge the Jews in the city to join with them in refraining from food as part of their direct appeal to God.

It has to be said that one way of increasing spiritual power in our lives, especially during a time of crisis, is to pray and fast. Sadly, although the Bible has so much to say about fasting, it is a subject that is rarely mentioned from modern-day pulpits.

Why is fasting so important? There are many reasons, of course, but one is this – when we eat, an increased amount of blood is needed to aid the digestive processes, but when we abstain from eating, a greater amount of blood is available to flow to our brains and aid our concentration. If you want to study the subject then I suggest you get hold of a good book on the matter, such as Arthur Wallis's *God's Chosen Fast*.

I know of no better way when facing a crisis, or when about to make a major life decision, than to refrain from making any decisions until you have entered into a time of prayer and fasting. Even a twenty-four hour period of fasting can bring tremendous spiritual results. But one word of caution: no fasting should be done without medical counsel if there are any physical ailments.

One way of increasing spiritual power in our lives is to pray and fast.

Father, are You trying to get my attention over this matter of fasting? Is this the voice of the Holy Spirit I hear? If so, help me be clear about the matter. Make me both willing and obedient. In Jesus' Name I pray. Amen.

THE ROYAL SCEPTRE

For Reading and Meditation: Esther 5:1–2

*"When he saw Queen Esther ... he ... held out to
her the gold sceptre ..." (v. 2)*

Esther's three days of prayer and fasting are over and now she comes to the moment when she has to approach the king. To come before the king uninvited could mean instant death. But Esther has already concluded that if her people are to be saved, there is no alternative. "If I perish, I perish," she says (4:16).

Although Esther has fasted and prayed, this does not relieve her of the need to approach the king personally. Some Christians think that when we pray and fast then God goes before us and relieves us of the responsibility to take action ourselves. Prayer and fasting sharpen our spiritual focus, and enable us to take the right and most effective action.

Esther, knowing the king's love of beauty, pays the closest attention to her appearance. Wearing the most beautiful apparel she can find, she slowly approaches the king. We do not know whether or not he was shocked to see her walk into his presence uninvited, but it is obvious he was overcome by her loveliness. The king holds out the gold sceptre to Esther – a sign that she is welcomed and accepted.

What a splendid picture this is of the way we sinners are accepted by the Almighty. God, we are told, has a "sceptre of righteousness" (Heb. 1:8, AV), which represents His purity and holiness. We are not pure enough to approach Him ourselves. However, dressed in the robe of righteousness which Christ provides, we are able to come before God, touch the sceptre of His burning purity which He holds out to us, and be welcomed into the divine presence as if we had never sinned. If that's not worth a Hallelujah, then I don't know what is!

*"If I perish,
I perish."*

Father, how can I sufficiently thank You that because of the shed blood of the Lord Jesus Christ I don't need an invitation to come into Your presence; I can stand before You at any time. What marvellous mercy. I am eternally grateful. Amen.

THE DIVINE STRATEGY

For Reading and Meditation: Esther 5:3–8

"If it pleases the king ... let the king, together with Haman, come today to a banquet ..." (v. 4)

K ing Xerxes is so overwhelmed by Esther's stunning beauty that even before she has time to explain why she has come into his presence uninvited, he says: "What is your request? Even up to half the kingdom, it will be given you" (v. 3). Esther, however, instead of immediately explaining the purpose of her visit, makes this proposal: "Will you and Haman attend a banquet later today?" Why this strange delaying tactic? Has she lost her nerve? Is she afraid to talk to the king about the real issue? No. The three days of prayer and fasting have sharpened her spiritual focus and she has come with a clear plan of action.

The king agrees to attend the banquet, and at the feast the king again asks Esther to state her request so that he may grant it to her. She declines to answer, but asks that the king and Haman attend another banquet the following day. Again, why this strange procedure? We are watching the wisdom of God at work, flowing through a human mind – always a marvellous thing to behold. As Esther waited before God in those three days of fasting, her thoughts were quietly taken over by God's thoughts. Her mind flowed into His mind and His mind flowed into her mind.

The wisdom of God at work.

How this illustrates the need to prayerfully soak our minds in the Word of God – daily. As I have told you many times before – human ingenuity and wisdom are utterly inadequate to meet the demands of daily living. If we are to live every day victoriously then we must spend more time with the Lord in prayer, and meditate on His Word. That is really the only place where we can exchange our thoughts for His.

O Father, forgive me for trying to battle against life in my own strength and with my own thoughts, when You are so willing to give me Your strength and Your thoughts. Help me organise my time so that I might spend more of it with You. In Jesus' Name. Amen.

For Reading and Meditation: Esther 5:9–14

"His wife Zeresh ... said ... 'Have a gallows built ... and ask the king in the morning to have Mordecai hanged on it' " (v. 14)

When Haman receives the news that he is invited to a special banquet arranged by Queen Esther, his joy knows no bounds. Arriving at the palace gates, however, and seeing Mordecai standing there so confidently, his joy leaves him. Haman thinks to himself once again: this rebellious Jew will not bow down before me. Restraining himself as best he can, he sits through the banquet, and later returns home to share the events of the day with his family.

"Just think of it," he tells his wife and friends, "today I was a special guest at the queen's banquet – no one else was present, but just the king and myself. Surely some new honour is being prepared for me." But there is one irritating note in the whole story, explains Haman: "Mordecai the Jew is still unwilling to bow before me." At this point Haman's wife, Zeresh, speaks up and says: "Don't let this miserable Jew spoil your existence. Build a gallows for him so that he may be hanged. And when you are with the king tomorrow morning, ask the king's permission to terminate his life. Then you will be rid of him for ever." "Excellent," says Haman, "that's exactly what I will do."

The power and influence that lies in the hands of a wife is tremendous – for good or evil. She has the ability to open a trap door through which her husband can fall to oblivion and despair, or erect a ladder by which he can climb to achievement and success. Blessed is the man with a good and godly wife who understands the power and influence that lies within her grasp and co-operates with the Almighty in making her husband the man God wants him to be.

The power and influence that lies in the hands of a wife is tremendous – for good or evil.

Gracious and loving heavenly Father, thank You for the power and influence that lies within every relationship – especially that of marriage. Help us use that power in the right way and for the right purposes. In Jesus' Name. Amen.

A SLEEPLESS NIGHT!

For Reading and Meditation: Esther 6:1–3

"'What honour and recognition has Mordecai received for this?' the king asked." (v. 3)

The great King Xerxes, despite his comfortable bed and luxurious surroundings, is unable to sleep! It has nothing to do with the food he has eaten at the banquet. God is at work in his life to see he is kept awake. We ought never to forget that the Almighty can reach into a human heart at any time. Remember how He came to the godless Belshazzar and, in the midst of his banquet hall, signalled the downfall of his kingdom by writing these startling words on the wall: "You have been weighed on the scales and found wanting" (Dan. 5:27).

King Xerxes does what most people do when they can't get to sleep – he looks for something to read. He calls for his servants to bring him the palace records and the chronicles of the court, only to find that, as he pores over the records of the past few months, there is an entry concerning the plot to assassinate the king. Xerxes en-quires whether or not the man who uncovered the plot – Mordecai – has been rewarded for this act of loyalty, and a search through the records shows that he has not. The king is somewhat surprised that no recognition has been given to Mordecai and plans to rectify the matter right away.

Can you see what is happening here? The hand of destiny is at work and the stage is being set for the last few scenes in the drama of God versus Haman. I heard a preacher say: "I feel sorry for anyone who tries to set out and involve himself in a programme that defiantly flies in the face of God." So do I. God wins every argument, every battle, and every cause. All the time!

God wins every argu-ment, every battle, and every cause. All the time!

O Father, the way Your power and wisdom combine to resolve problems is so awesome and astonishing. Why do I tremble so much before my problems when I have such a God as this? Forgive and help me come through to a greater trust. In Jesus' Name. Amen.

INDESTRUCTIBLE!

For Reading and Meditation: Esther 6:4–14

*"Since Mordecai ... is of Jewish origin ...
you will surely come to ruin!" (v. 13)*

As the sun rises over the great Persian empire, Haman awakens with a tremendous sense of optimism and well-being. "Today", he muses, "the king will most probably give me a great honour and then I shall be in a position to rid myself for ever of the man I most hate – Mordecai the Jew." Having given his carpenters orders to build a gallows, on which he plans to hang Mordecai, he makes his way to the palace.

He arrives there just at the moment when the king is looking for someone to advise him on what kind of a reward to give to Mordecai for uncovering the plot to assassinate him. King Xerxes says to Haman: "What should be done for the man the king delights to honour?" (v. 6). Haman, not knowing what the king has in mind and believing this to be a reference to himself, suggests: "Let him be king for a day. Let the royal robes be brought ... let him ride the king's horse and let him wear a golden crown." "Excellent," says the king, "go at once and do everything you propose for Mordecai the Jew." Can you imagine Haman's feelings as, in obedience to the king's command, he has to go to Mordecai, assist him to mount the king's horse, and then lead him through the city, calling on all to respect the man whom the king has decided to honour?

Shamed and humiliated, Haman returns to his home, morally and politically defeated. There his advisers pronounce the significant words of our text for today. These are indeed solemn and powerful words, and they have as much force today as they did then. Those who seek to completely destroy the people called the Jews must first destroy God.

Those who seek to completely destroy the people called the Jews must first destroy God.

Father, this is not only true of Your people, the Jews, it is also true of Your redeemed people, the Church. To destroy me the devil would first have to destroy You. This means I am undefeatable and indestructible. Blessed be Your wonderful Name. Amen.

THE GROAN OF GOD

For Reading and Meditation: Esther 7:1–10

"If it pleases your majesty, grant me my life …
And spare my people …" (v. 3)

No doubt Haman, having suffered so much shame and humiliation, would have preferred to have stayed at home rather than attend the queen's second banquet. He knows, however, that to ignore her invitation would only add to his difficulties. So, licking his wounds, he makes his way to the royal affair. As the banquet proceeds, the king, eager to hear Esther's request, again invites her to make it known, adding that he favours her so greatly he is prepared to give her half his kingdom. Esther, sensing that this is the moment when the issue has to be faced, begins to quietly disclose her Jewish identity, her relationship to Mordecai, and her deep concern at how the king's edict, if it is allowed to take effect, will annihilate her and her people.

Her intercession is a model which all Christians would do well to emulate. She is bold, plain, simple and direct. She identifies herself with the Jewish people and humbly pleads for their deliverance.

As Esther intercedes most powerfully for the lives of her people, the king is deeply moved. He is not aware at this time of Haman's plans to annihilate the Jews, presumably because Haman has taken great care to conceal the intent of the new law. So he asks: "Who is he? Where is the man who has dared to do such a thing?" Esther answers: "The adversary and enemy is this vile Haman" (vv. 5–6). The king is so angry at this discovery that he retires to the garden to reflect on the situation. While he is there, Haman throws himself at Queen Esther's feet to plead for his life. Esther is reclining on the couch, and when the king returns and sees Haman crouching at her feet he assumes that he is attempting to seduce his wife and orders his immediate death. One of the king's chamberlains, hearing this, suggests that Haman be executed on the gallows built for Mordecai.

Esther's intercession is a model which all Christians would do well to emulate.

O Father, I am so thankful for the way the truths of Your Word feed my spirit. Day by day I can feel them penetrating to the core of my being. Nothing is purposeless and nothing can work against You. Blessed be Your wonderful Name. Amen.

THE UNDEFEATABLE GOD

For Reading and Meditation: Esther 8:1–17

"The king took off his signet ring ... reclaimed from Haman, and presented it to Mordecai." (v. 2)

With Haman dead, a new day is about to dawn in the great empire of Persia. Esther, recognising that this is the right moment to introduce her foster-father, Mordecai, to the king, brings him with her into the king's presence. When the king sees for the first time the man who saved his life, he is filled with delight and proceeds at once to elevate him to a high position in the land. Now the Almighty, instead of having just one of His people set up in a strategic position in Persia, has two. But just listen to this and tell me if there is no humour in the Bible. Mordecai receives from the king the ring that once belonged to Haman and is appointed as the manager of Haman's estate.

The one thing that makes all of God's plans undefeatable, of course, is His foreknowledge. Because He sees everything that is going to happen in the future, He is able to anticipate events and out-manoeuvre whatever may be contrary to His purposes. Satan does not possess foreknowledge. He probably has a good deal of intuition, and a keen sense of anticipation, but he cannot foresee the future in the way God can. This is quite clear from the events that took place at the cross. Satan thought he had brought Christ down into death, but found that the very thing he planned would defeat Christ – the cross – actually contributed to His greatest victory.

> *God alone knows the end from the beginning.*

What does all this say to us? It says that you can go out into the day knowing that God has foreseen every trick that the devil may use upon you, and outwit and out-manoeuvre him in a way that will enrich your life and bring glory to Christ's Name. God alone knows the end from the beginning. Never forget that!

Father, I am consoled by the thought that You and You alone know the end from the beginning. Though Satan is obviously a being of great power and ability, he is clearly no match for You. I am so grateful. Amen.

For Reading and Meditation: Esther 9:1–22

"Mordecai ... sent letters to all the Jews ...
to have them celebrate annually ..." (vv. 20–21)

The substance of the new law, introduced to modify the effects of the original edict to annihilate the Jews, was simply this – all Jews could, by every means possible, take up their own defence. When finally the dreaded execution day arrives, those who set out to execute the Jews find themselves in disarray. A strange fear has fallen upon the persecutors, and many of the officers of the Persian army, instead of executing the Jews, do everything they can to save them.

Back in the palace, the king invites Esther to make one more request of him, whereupon she asks him to put to death Haman's ten sons. This request seems hardly in keeping with Esther's gentle nature, but we must remember that she is acting here as the representative of God in what we call judicial execution. God wanted to emphasise that it is pointless to try to liquidate His people, and it was He who prompted Esther to make this request. In all, 75,000 Persians died on the day when it was expected that many thousands of Jews would be annihilated. Following this great day of deliverance, Mordecai makes moves to establish it as an annual memorial throughout all generations. Now, some 2,500 years later, Jews celebrate the event every year in a feast which they call the Feast of Purim.

Christians have a special memorial too. It is called the "table of communion", a simple but meaningful ceremony which God has established in the Church to remind us of that glorious day at Calvary when Satan's plans were wrecked, and salvation was made available to all humanity. May that memorial become more meaningful to us every time we participate in it.

An annual memorial throughout all generations.

O Father, I see that while the Jews have something to celebrate, I have something more significant. Your deliverance for me on the cross is a spiritual deliverance, not merely a physical one. May the wonder of it sink deeper and deeper within me. In Jesus' Name I pray. Amen.

VICTORY EVERY DAY

For Reading and Meditation: Esther 9:23–10:3

"Mordecai the Jew was second in rank to King Xerxes …" (10:3)

The thrilling story of Esther ends with Mordecai being firmly established as Prime Minister of Persia. Historians tell us that under Mordecai's management, the land grew strong and prosperous. He was the right man in the right place at the right time.

As you cast your mind back over the ground on which we have travelled these past weeks, does not the sovereignty of God appear in a more awesome light than ever before? Remind yourself that nothing, absolutely nothing, can defeat or frustrate the purposes of God. Many things appear beyond hope or irretrievable to us, but nothing is irretrievable to God. He who knows how to take occasion from Adam's fall and bring in such a perfect redemption, may be safely trusted with every event and every action of history – good or bad. Let this thought sink into your soul throughout every hour of this day – our God reigns!

The Jews, in looking back over their history, give thanks to God for those occasions when He worked in great power to effect their deliverance. In honour of those events they set aside special dates and seasons. But such is the breathtaking wonder of God's grace to believers that really there are just not enough days to go round. When, after World War II, Europe celebrated victory over the Nazis, they called it VE Day – Victory in Europe. Some years later, a boy was asked by his history teacher what VE Day stood for. He replied: "Victory Every Day". Well, that is not what it means, but it is certainly what it can mean. In the light of God's sovereignty and love, we who are His redeemed children can live out our lives in full assurance of certain victory – this day and every day.

Our God reigns!

Father, let my consciousness be filled with the thought that the same loving sovereignty and care which went into the planning of Ruth and Esther's life is also at work in mine. Help me never forget that no matter what happens, You are always on Your throne. Amen.